PASTOR TRUMAN L. CARTER'S

Soul Searching Sermons

STEVEN W. EDWARDS

Copyright © 2017 Steven W. Edwards

All rights reserved. All rights reserved All rights reserved. No part of this book may be reproduced by any mechanical, photographic, or electronic process, or in the form of phonographic recording without prior consent of publisher.

Liberation's Publishing LLC ~ West Point, MS. 39773

Scriptures are taken from the Authorized King James Version of the Holy Bible.

ISBN-978-1-7320846-2-9

Dedication

This book of Sermons is dedicated to the memory of two men, my sons, Truman L. Carter II and Richard H. Carter. May they both rest in peace, because their work down here is done. I have written their biography in the back.

Pastor Carter L. Truman

TABLE OF CONTENTS

Introduction 11

God's House 15

Why Go To Church 17

Everything Changes 19

Everything Changes Part 2 21

The Power of God 23

Christian's Don't Quit 25

A Real Christian 27

Faithful to God 29

Fundamental Faith 31

Ponder The Cross 33

The Purpose of Christ 35

Five Kings In Church 37

Beware Of These Kings 39

Troubled World 41

The fellowship Of God 43

Who Should We Pray For 45

Grace and Faith 49

A Mother Hen and Her Chicks 51

Salvation and Your Family 53

Killing A Church 55

Smarter Than A Pharisees 57

Does god Need A Mule 59

Homecoming 61

Common Sense 63

21st Century 67

Living Daily 69

Heart Of Stone 71

No Time Zone 75

Eased But Not Grieved 79

The touch Of Jesus 83

Why I Love Jesus 85

The hour of Death 89

All I have For God	93
Christian Talent	97
Death Angel	99
It's Time	103
Our Mind	107
Alleluia	109
Why Was Jesus Born	113
Ways To Miss Heaven	115
New Year's Vow	119
Three Precious Jewels	123
When the Shadows Gathers	125
Encouragement	129
The ABC's of Jesus	133
Last Judgement	137
Ask Yourself	141

Steven W. Edwards

John 6:63 It is the spirit that quickeneth; the flesh profiteth nothing: the words that I speak unto you, they are spirit, and they are life.

INTRODUCTION

God through the eyes of Truman Carter. This book is going to try and show you God through Pastor Truman Carter's eyes. This is a book like no other. It has something in it that will touch everyone from young to old. In life most of our problems are somewhat the same. We are all sinners trying to stay out of hell. Maybe after reading this book you will find that path that leads to Jesus. Following and Trusting him is the only way to heaven. You must follow and trust him to the very end. As a sinner myself I can tell you it isn't easy, but it is the only way.

We're going to tell you things that happened in our life for following God and what happened from not following him. We will also share of people in the bible who did the same things. My name is Steven Wayne Edwards, and those that know me know I was in the world for a long time. Only by the Grace of God did I come back to God. Because of this I was able to help with this book. I can tell people about wrong turns and bad choices I made. I hope that by sharing my mistakes I can keep someone else from making the same mistakes.

I pray that this book leads someone to Christ. If only one person gets saved after reading this book it will be well worth the effort. If God can use someone like me to carry his word to the lost he can use anyone of you. You can never get too far in the world that God cannot get you out. When it comes to you, God will get your attention one way or the other.

I ran from God a long time. One day I was driving and my brakes went out. I literally hit the church I was running from. I don't run from God anymore. My pastor, Truman Carter, brings God's word and I write it down and pass it out wherever I go. If people won't go to church I'll bring the church to them.

So just sit back, and let God work as you are reading this book. There are almost a hundred different messages in here. If you can find just one that helps you find Jesus our job is done. I hope this helps you grow closer to the Lord. I want to thank God for giving me a chance to bring his word. I hope you have as much joy reading this as we did working on it. Pastor Truman Carter and Steven Wayne Edwards working for God the only way we know how!

Steven W. Edwards

GOD'S HOUSE

This place we come to and worship is the house of God. There is no place like this in town. This is not a dance hall or a place to buy booze. It is a house of God. If you get happy about going to the beer store, but fuss about going to church you need to pray. If you are not sick or dead, God expects you to be at his house.

We come to church for sanctification of the saints, to love one another, forsake not the love of God. We do not want to destroy but lift up. If you love God you will keep his commandments. Where can you get sanctification outside of church. You cannot put faith in money or the bank. You cannot trust the people in office, because they are lovers of pleasure and not lovers of God.

There are probably thousands of people on the

beach today, but the house of God is almost empty. You need to be where the house of God is. The church provides sanctification to your soul. When the doors of the church are open the members should be able to count on you being there. Most importantly God should be able to count on you being there. Do you love God and his church? Are you willing to put everything aside when it comes time to come to church? It's a sad world we live in. We are on time for everything, but God. What if God did us like that? He isn't. He is on time for all of our problems. We should start being on time for him!

Why Go To Church

Why Go to church when the fish are biting, or there's a great race going on? It may be that you just don't feel like going today. Hebrews 10:25 says forsake not the gather of ourselves together as the manner of some, but exhorting one another and so much more as you see the day approaching."

How can I tell you about the word of God if you're not here? Jesus also knew the house of God was important. John 2:14-16 says "and found in the temple those that sold oxen and sheep and doves, and the changers of money sitting:

15 and when he had made a scourge of small cords, he drove them all out of the temple, and the sheep, and the oxen; and poured out the changers' money, and overthrew the tables; 16 and said unto them that sold doves, Take these things hence; make not my Father's

house an house of merchandise."

Did Peter and John think it was important to go into the house of the Lord? If they hadn't gone they would not have seen the lame man walk. They would not have been able to share in that. David longed for home not just to get back to his kingdom or his wife and family. Psalms 122:1 I was glad when they said unto me, Let us go into the house of the LORD."

Besides being saved, going to church is the most important thing you can do. Jesus told Peter in Matthew 16:18 And I say also unto thee, That thou art Peter, and upon this rock I will build my church; and the gates of hell shall not prevail against it."

Two or three times a week we can be with God in his house. To be known by Jesus and God the father is one of the greatest gifts you will ever have. Don't put God second. Don't just come to his house when there's nothing else to do.

EVERYTHING CHANGES

Everything in this world changes even darkness. In the bathroom when you cut on the light darkness leaves. Nothing ever stays the same, but the way we are born into the world, death, and hell will never change. Heaven is still the sweetest place we can think about and can go to.

Is hell outdated? The reality of hell is such a dreaded place. Revelation 1:18 says, I am he that liveth, and was dead; and, behold, I am alive for evermore, Amen; and have the keys of hell and of death." Jesus mentioned hell nine times. If there is no hell there is no heaven. The bible speaks of both.

If this nation has stopped believing in Jesus we are a nation lost and without hope. What has darkness have to do with light? How does anyone with Christ sit down with someone without Christ and fix any problems. We are supposed to be in the bible belt. Look at how we act. I don't believe Hurricane Katrina was an accident. It was a message from God for all the lost people. Things in this world might change, but hell does not change. It is still a place for the wicked.

God doesn't want any to go to hell, but if we do not turn our hearts to him that is where we will surely go! Luke 16:19-31 tells how the rich man had it all on Earth, but would not give a man called Lazarus, who was a beggar, as much as a drink of water or anything to eat while on Earth. The rich man never thought about hell on earth. He had the money to do whatever he wanted here. When he died he had nothing, no money, no power.

Are you a real Christian? Will you be among the few that will go to heaven? Will you be like the rich man and let heaven pass you by. You can have everything you think you need on earth just like the rich man, but how when the rich man got to hell how he begged. It was too late for him. It's not too late for you yet. You're not dead. Just don't wait too long!

Everything Changes Part 2

Matthew 7:13-14 says, Enter ye in at the strait gate: for wide is the gate, and broad is the way, that leadeth to destruction, and many there be which go in thereat: 14 Because strait is the gate, and narrow is the way, which leadeth unto life, and few there be that find it.

The devil cares nothing about you. God cares nothing about your body He loves your soul. God is going to give you a new body. When you die, you're going to have to give up your earthly body. The devil wants your soul.

The region of hell, where is it? Amos 9:2 says, Though they dig into hell, thence shall mine hand take them; though they climb up to heaven, thence will I bring them down:" Somewhere beneath us is fire and brimstone.

You cannot see the soul. You only see what is on the outside. You can never see me, this body is just my house. You cannot see the breath of God. We must worship God as he is. He is our breath and truth. Where will your soul go, to the Lord or to hell? There is no paradise when you open your eyes after you die. You will open them in heaven or hell.

The regret of hell no one will rejoice over. They will regret every hour of everyday. It will be a reminder that Jesus came and gave his life. Once you are in hell you will have all your senses alive. You will be able to hear, feel, speak, and remember.

Hell is not outdated. This is why people are going there every day. We should not wait until we ae in hell to worry about telling someone about Jesus. Tell people now and you and them can avoid hell all the way around!

The Power of God

You have got the power of God behind you, and Satan does not have it. Hold your head up. Don't walk around looking sad, because whatever you're going through the power of God is with you. Keep fighting the good fight for God. Keep living for God.

Christians I'm telling you hold on just a little longer. Don't quit. Heaven is so close at hand. The Holy Spirit shapes and molds what we say and gives it to God. This is why we have help in everything we do. We are too far in debt to God to turn back now. You have a job to do and it's not easy. God wants you to do it anyway. There are no quitters in the army of the Lord. Get out and fight a good fight for God.

You've been talked about and laughed at, but you still did your job. The next day you're ready to do it all again. You will be able to spit in the devil's eye. Let them talk about you good or bad. Just keep fighting the good fight. Just tell the devil you are not going to win. "I will not throw in the towel."

It doesn't matter what I'm going through. I will not quit on God. I have come too far. Romans 1:16 " For I am not ashamed of the gospel of Christ: for it is the power of God unto salvation to everyone that believeth; to the Jew first, and also to the Greek."

God wants you to keep going, and keep looking at him. BE not afraid, because you are working for God and you have all power.

CHRISTIAN'S DON'T QUIT

Jeremiah 20:7-9 says, "O Lord, thou hast deceived me, and I was deceived; thou art stronger than I, and hast prevailed: I am in derision daily, every one mocketh me. (8) For since I spake, I cried out, I cried violence and spoil; because the word of the Lord was made a reproach unto me, and a derision, daily. (9) Then I said, I will not make mention of him, nor speak any more in his name. But his word was in mine heart as a burning fire shut up in my bones, and I was weary with forbearing, and I could not stay."

A Christian called by God will not quit. When it seems no one cares, or you've had enough it's easy to feel that way. No matter what you cannot quit or turn back. Our calling is a high calling. We have a holy calling. You were saved to fight the good fight for God.

No one promised you a bed of roses. The world

doesn't take to kindly to people that carry the message for Jesus. No one promised you would always get what you wanted. No one promised it would not be hard, or that you wouldn't have problems. God did promise that he would always be there.

The word will keep us in his glory, and in his arms. Do you know how much book work that would be if God took our name out of the book of life every time we messed up? You were dead in sin. Now you are on your way to heaven. You are working on your way to heaven. You are working for God so do not quit.

You have a cloud of witnesses. These are the angels that have passed on. They are cheering us on in heaven. They are saying fight that good fight. You can do it. When you are down all you need is a dose of Holy Spirit. That will get you started again. The price is too high. Jesus paid for it. He paid his life so we could be forgiven of our sins. We do not have to go to hell. He got the keys to heaven, and he is waiting to unlock the door for you!

A Real Christian

Can you find a real Christian? The word Christian is found three times in the bible. You can tell a Christian by the fruit they bare. Most Christians today do not bare good fruit. Some do not produce any fruit for God at all. They turn away those in need.

It's easy to say I'm a Christian, but a person that goes to a bars and then comes to church is questionable. Will we live by the milk of the word of God. Some Christians live their whole life on milk. They are the ones that need to keep their mouth shut.

I won't give a dime for some of the preachers or some of these so called Christians. You cannot run around with dope heads and walk how they walk. We need to be set apart. Show me a real Christian. Being a Christian is not easy. I'm one right down to the bottom of my soul. If you think you are the only one that is going to heaven you are a fool. If you are a Christian why are you doing what the world does?

Fear no man only God. He can destroy the body and the soul. I hope when you die your family can say he or she was a real Christian.

FAITHFUL TO GOD

God does not care about big numbers. If he did he would not have only chosen twelve apostles. Jesus and the woman at the well one on one. The blind man on the road, and the blind man at the pool of Siloam were with Jesus one on one. Jesus told his disciples let not your heart be weary. I will go prepare a place for you, in my father's house there are many mansions. If it were not so I would not have told you so.

Acts 20:20-21 says, "And how I kept back nothing that was profitable unto you, but have shewed you, and have taught you publicly, and from house to house, (21) Testifying both to the Jews, and also to the Greeks, repentance toward God, and faith toward our Lord Jesus Christ.

Romans 12:1-2 says, "I beseech you therefore, brethren, by the mercies of God, that ye present your bodies a living sacrifice, holy, acceptable unto God, which is your reasonable service.

(2) And be not conformed to this world: but be ye transformed by the renewing of your mind, that ye may prove what is that good, and acceptable, and perfect, will of God."

Romans 12:12-13 says, "Rejoicing in hope; patient in tribulation; continuing instant in prayer; (13) Distributing to the necessity of saints; given to hospitality."

What is God's will in your life? Is it like Paul because he was faithful in soul winning? Are we faithful in winning souls and are we faithful to God?

Fundamental Faith

Jude 1:3 says, "Beloved, when I gave all diligence to write unto you of the common salvation, it was needful for me to write unto you, and exhort you that ye should earnestly contend for the faith which was once delivered unto the saints."

2 Timothy 3:15-17, "And that from a child thou hast known the holy scriptures, which are able to make thee wise unto salvation through faith which is in Christ Jesus. (16) All scripture is given by inspiration of God, and is profitable for doctrine, for reproof, for correction, for instruction in righteousness: (17) That the man of God may be perfect, thoroughly furnished unto all good works.

Fundamental faith is a faith that believes in the word of God. A fundamental faith is faith that believes that God's word has inspiration in word of the bible. Today we have men pleasers that change the bible to the way that they want it read. Revelation 2:4-5 says, "Nevertheless I have somewhat against thee, because thou hast left thy first love. (5) Remember therefore from whence thou art fallen, and repent, and do the first works; or else I will come unto thee quickly, and will remove thy candlestick out of his place, except thou repent.

The scripture is saying if you keep living in sin and not change God will withdraw his blessing from you. God knows we are going to do wrong, but if your heart is cold God will withdraw his blessing from you. When you go to the house of God you can serve him and enjoy yourself.

You can read about faith and talk about faith, but before you die you better have faith in God. If you not you will see hell first hand. Then you will see why God is so important to you. God's joy is so sweet if you will just turn to him and see.

PONDER THE CROSS

Words cannot express the feeling that was suffered on the cross. The pondering of the cross of Christ, the physical pain that Christ had to go through and the misunderstanding of the cross. Most people there didn't even know who Jesus was. They didn't know why he was there. Some said to Jesus, "Do you not fear God?" Another one asked, "If you be the Christ come down from the cross and save yourself."

One of the men on the cross with Jesus said to him, "Lord remember me." Jesus responded, "This day you will be in paradise with me." Jesus knew he was doomed to death. He did not worry, because he knew he had power over death. Both of the men on the cross were sinners, but one of them saw there was hope beyond this world. He saw it on the cross. His name was Jesus.

He was like no other person in this world. God sent him to die on the cross for us, but just like some of the people today and back then there was some confusion at the cross of who Jesus was and why he did not come down off the cross. God had a plan that he would send his son to die for all the worlds sins.

One of the men on the cross honored God and said this man has done nothing, yet he is on the cross with us. When Jesus was on the cross he was not sinless, because he had our sins on his back. Because of this sin God turned his back on his son and let him die on that cross. There was a roman soldier watching Jesus and saw the darkness that fell over them after his death and said surely this was a man of God. Great fear fell upon him.

THE PURPOSE OF CHRIST

Peter saw the blood of Christ and the purpose of Christ and followed Christ all the way to the cross. The hour before he said he never knew him, Peter followed Jesus everywhere he went. He heard Jesus tell of things that were about to come and he heard Jesus preach the Gospel, and he talked about heaven and earth. When Jesus was hung on the cross Peter knew that the scripture was true and had to be fulfilled.

Jesus loved us so much that he put all he did in a book so we could read the word of God. So we could learn how to live our life right. We could read it when we wanted to. Paul said should we give glory and save the message of the cross. When I think about the cross I see the poor and the rich right there.

In the crowd I see me. Where you there when they

crucified my Lord? I was born into this world into sin, but one day on the cross Jesus called my name. Have you pondered the cross?

Matthew 27:45-46 tells us, "Now from the sixth hour there was darkness over all the land unto the ninth hour.

46 And about the ninth hour Jesus cried with a loud voice, saying, Eli, Eli, lama sabachthani? that is to say, My God, my God, why hast thou forsaken me?"

Five Kings In Church

Concerning the Kings of Canaan the book of Joshua says, 10:22-27, "Then said Joshua, Open the mouth of the cave, and bring out those five kings unto me out of the cave. (23) And they did so, and brought forth those five kings unto him out of the cave, the king of Jerusalem, the king of Hebron, the king of Jarmuth, the king of Lachish, and the king of Eglon. (24) And it came to pass, when they brought out those kings unto Joshua, that Joshua called for all the men of Israel, and said unto the captains of the men of war which went with him, Come near, put your feet upon the necks of these kings. And they came near, and put their feet upon the necks of them.

(25) And Joshua said unto them, Fear not, nor be dismayed, be strong and of good courage: for thus shall the Lord do to all your enemies against whom ye fight. (26) And afterward Joshua smote them, and slew them,

and hanged them on five trees: and they were hanging upon the trees until the evening. (27) And it came to pass at the time of the going down of the sun, that Joshua commanded, and they took them down off the trees, and cast them into the cave wherein they had been hid, and laid great stones in the cave's mouth, which remain until this very day."

BEWARE OF THESE KINGS

The first, King Light Foot is smooth, and he will persuade you to tone it down and give up the gift God has given you. The second, King Compromise, it does not matter what has to be done he will compromise everything to make people happy. In the bible Jesus did not tell us to compromise what was right just to make people happy. We need to watch out for this king, but we do not need to compromise when it comes to the word of God.

The third king, Clare, he is quick to condemn those that he thinks don't measure up. He always wants to set us straight when we do not believe like he does. No matter what there is only one way to be saved and that is by the blood of Jesus. The fourth king, Freedom, he will always brag. He has the gift to boast. They are happy in church while everything is going good, but as soon as things start going bad they will always go someplace else. When you are saved you need to find a church home and not move. You can also call them preacher lovers. As soon as it gets tough they will leave.

The fifth king, Decline, goes under all kinds of names. His duty is to rob you of your liberty and he will rob you of serving God. As we look around salvation is the same as with Peter and James and with God. No matter what God loves people. God uses people every day in life. What is church and what does it mean to you? King Decline can also be the king of discouragement. A king with no heart and has robbed more people of being saved than anyone of the other kings. All he wants is to discourage anyone he can for being saved and living their life for Jesus. If you see any of these kings please stay far away. There is only trouble ahead.

TROUBLED WORLD

We live in a troubled world where all we hear is bad news. In the newspaper or on TV you rarely meet someone today without them telling you about some kind of bad news. We have hope. God is our light, and God is the one that will give us all we need. God will not hold back any good thing from his children.

We have the faithfulness of God to keep us safe. God can be trusted, but you cannot trust a lot of people in this world. We live in a greedy world, and people do not care about you. People just want their pockets fat. We cannot trust the men in office to do what they are supposed to do.

We pay taxes, but our roads aren't fixed. We cannot trust most of the people in this world. We cannot trust the things of the world, but we can always count on

God. Christians, do not say you are lucky just say you are blessed. You have the word of God to show you the right way to live. That is what we must go by each and everyday . The kings and some of the wars and some of the wars and some of your family members have passed on. The word of God will not.

You can be a part of any and all kinds of churches, but it is not what is in the church but what is in the heart of the people at church. There are places where the true word of God is not being preached. You might make people mad or stir things up. People might not like you. So what, God loves you. That is all that counts. Do not let someone else run your life by their words.

THE FELLOWSHIP OF GOD

The fellowship of the Saints of God, nothing is more refreshing than being with other believers, brothers, and sisters of Christ. We are closer than our earthly brother and sisters because our earthly family will dissolve along with the things of this world. Everything bound and in heaven will be perfect.

God is with us all the way to the end. He is in us. In God's eyes we are perfect. We know the Lord Jesus is with us. We have the blessed help of the Lord to inspire us and to let us know we have the spirit of God. It saves us in the time of trouble.

The Christian life is not to be live in in the fleshed, but in the spirit, for the honor of God. Just think about it if it was not for the father there would not be a son. Without the Son of God there would not be a cross.

Without the cross there would not be forgiveness for our sins.

Nothing happens unless it first goes by the father, because every person has the breather of God in them saved or not. It is called a soul. If you have not done it already you need to let God into your soul. He will change your life. You do not want to miss your one trip to heaven and end up in hell. The devil will always try to keep you down. God has his Saints to lift you up when you are down. One day when you get to heaven you will know all things.

WHO SHOULD WE PRAY FOR

Who should we pray for. The bible says there are certain people to pray for. We must first pray for ourselves, but always pray for others. If you cannot pray for others then Christ is not in us. We need to pray for all men and women. If we know someone is troubled. We need to pray for them.

In God's eyes all colors of people are the same. The same breath you breathe and all was made by God. About 97% of the people above us are not honest. So before you cast them down do you pray? It is alright not to agree with someone. If you did not vote sit down and shut up. Pray for your enemy and love him. You can believe in God, but if you do not accept him in your heart you will go to hell.

Pray for the sick. God's people should listen to the

troubles of others. We should try to help them. We should not tell anyone else about it. If the person has some troubles that you cannot solve or if that person is sick you should let them call for the elders of the church.

Pray for Israel. It is in a hot bed. The USA is surrounded by waters we are not in danger where we are. We are blessed. God says whoever blesses Israel I will bless them. Do you pray for Israel? They are God's chosen people. The battle of Armageddon is going to be somewhere around Israel. Pray for all the Saints. People owe certain things to each other. We need to pray for each other when we need prayer. Pray for the Ministers.

Pray for what is going on in our country. We have a bunch of scared wimps preaching God's word. They are scared of losing their money form the people at church. They are men pleasers. What about preachers that will get up and preach in blue jeans and saddles. To me that is very disrespectful to God.

So come and start doing what God says to do. Do not worry about the world or money. If God put a message on your heart you would be wise to tell the people what they need to hear. People want a young preacher and his new ways, but there is only one way to the cross. Preachers do not sell yourself short just to make people happy. There are too many souls at stake. Do you really want their blood on your hands for not preaching the word?

Steven W. Edwards

GRACE AND FAITH

By grace and faith we are saved and only by God's power. We cannot boast about it. If we could earn it there would be many people who think they are saved. Jesus called a lot of people in his day hypocrites. There is not one that is good. Yet still we judge. The one that is saved God will say "Welcome In!"

Jesus has already gone to heaven. He has already built us mansions. God has given us the promise of death. Death for a child of God is great. We can say we are forgiven by the blood of Jesus Christ. He did not deserved to die, we did. He took our place. Not any of the good deeds we have done or any reward for us, it was given us by grace. God's word is true.

God's words are true and will never leave us . We are part of Christ and hall his glory. After all the pain in this world God will tell Jesus to come and bring his children home. We will be in heaven with our maker. Not all my family members can say that because all of them are not saved. The hardest people to witness to is your family. They know you and know everything you have done. They sometimes think about your past life and not your present. They sometimes cannot see that God has made a change. Your family should be the easiest for you to lead to Christ. Ask God to give you the words to say. If you know you are saved don't worry about what others might say.

A Mother Hen and Her Chicks

It is amazing how a mother hen calls her chicks. They will come running. A mother hen will put herself in harm's way to take care of her chicks. It is amazing how the babies know their mother. It is the same way the children of God should know our father. There is a warning call that the mother puts out. When it starts to rain or when danger comes she will put her chicks under her wings. Let the other animals kill her instead of her chicks.

The same way Jesus died for us so we would not have to go to hell. God speaks our name and we walk with him. The shelter call tells the chicks to hide from the thing that is trying to do the harm. In times like this Jesus is our shelter.

Then there is a following call. This tells the chicks to follow her. That is the same way we need to follow the

Lord in all that we do . It is not always a party or a good time. It might be hard but we need to follow him.

The feeding call tells her chicks it is time to eat. The feeding call for us is Jesus and he is he bread of life. When our souls are hungry we need to get fed so it might grow. Are you strong enough in the word to lead others to Christ. The warmth call tells her chicks it's time to go to bed. When it gets night for us is when God calls us home. He doesn't call just me but all the believers in the world!

Salvation and Your Family

Salvation of your family it's what everyone wants, their family to be saved. People don't realize how important it is for them to be saved. Sooner or later if you are saved your family will be saved. Noah built the ark for the saving of his family. It would be terrible for us to go to heaven and our family members go to hell. What if one of your children end up in hell and they ask you why you didn't tell them about heaven.

Open up your bible and read it to your family. Abraham was faithful to God and God promised to give him more children than the stars in the sky. Even though he was in his 90's he would have many children. Abraham and his entire family was blessed.

What is more important to you than your family. Your family can be touched by the way you are living.

There is nothing more rewarding than seeing your child do good just by following your footsteps. It's a blessing to know your child is telling someone about Jesus, or just to know when your family member closes their eyes for the last time their soul will go to Jesus.

About a third of the parents I know do not go to church. It is sad not to know if your family members are saved. It is the man's job to tell their family it is time for church. Look how far we have come away from the church in this generation. Time is passing for this world and their sins, but God's promises never wear out. If you believe in the Lord Jesus Christ you will be saved. Don't wait too long because time is running out. You need to turn to God. Acts 16:31 says, "Believe on the Lord Jesus Christ and you will be saved. You and your household."

KILLING A CHURCH

How do you think you can kill a church? You can kill a church by staying away. When the main organ of the body, which is the heart, is taken away or if it stops beating death will come. It is the same with the church. If the members stop going to church it will die. We do not go to church the benefit of one another. God misses his children when they do not come to church. The word is the bread of life, but if we do not go to church we starve for not having our food. The church only lives by growing and if it stops growing it will die.

The key to growing a church is it must be filled with the Holy Spirit before anything will ever happen. You only get things right in your life by going to church not by staying away. There are people in the church that will leave the church when things are bad. Do not let that discourage you.

Heaven and Earth will pass away, but God's words will stand. You kill a church by staying a babe in Christ. Grow in the word and do not stay away from it. You can kill a church by being selfish. The money that people spend foolishly we could use to reach the whole world. We are new creatures in Christ. We should be different from the world. People will call us odd. Jesus washed his disciples feet to show he was no better than them. Real worship is letting the Holy Spirit work in your heart, because the Holy Spirit might give you the word one way and to me another way. Either way the word will lift you up!

SMARTER THAN A PHARISEES

Are you smarter than a Pharisee? Are churches today filled with modern day Pharisees? The Pharisees were the most church going people. They went to church more than the people do today. Just because you have a membership to a church does not mean you are going to heaven.

If you are depending on that it is like you are standing on a board with oil on it and you are sliding to hell. The Pharisees worked for their church. We all need to work for our church and pray a prayer from our heart. When the heart stops the rest of the body is dead. The breath in your body is called your soul.

The breath is just lent to you by God. One day you can give it back to him through the blood of Jesus. If you don't give your breath back to God you will end up in hell. Preachers you do not have to preach about tithing too much, because if their heart is right with God they will tithe. They will do it because they love God and not because they automatically should tithe.

If you give ten percent of and an offering then he will bless you so much you will not be able to count them. If you love the Lord you will give. When it is time for you to go out of this world it all comes down to one thing. You must be born again. Are you smarter than a Pharisee? They turned their back on Jesus. They let him die on a cross because they said he was wrong. If you are born again, I say you are smarter than a Pharisee.

Does God Need A Mule

Does God need a mule to speak to you. Has it ever been a time you started to go somewhere and had a flat. Most likely if you got in that car, got down the road, and the tire blew out you may be in a bad car wreck. So the Lord always knows what is best for you. Have you ever said Lord why is this happening to me now? I tell you there is nothing in life that happens without God already knowing it. God needs a mule to talk to you before you can listen. Nothing in life happens without God already knowing it was going to happen, or God having his hand in it.

We need money to live in our lives, but money is not everything. Since you were a child how many times has God turned his back on you. The devil puts in our minds things we want, but not that we need. What does it take for God to get through to you. The only salvation for this country is for God's people to pray.

Why are you so busy that you do not let your light shine. When God said love one another he meant that. When he said I will be with you always even to death that is what he meant. Numbers 22:30 says, "So the donkey said to Balaam am I not your donkey on which you have ridden ever since I became yours to this day? Was I ever disposed to do this for you? And he said no."

Does it take a donkey to speak to you before you will obey God. If God did send a donkey to speak to you would you listen or try to run away? What if there was an angel in front of you with a sword, would you keep going on and get your head cut off or would you turn around and listen to the donkey?

Homecoming

Homecoming is a token of honor. It is looking back and thanking the people before you. If the people before us had not stood and fought there would not have been a church. We should also stand and fight the good fight. We should go to church and get a blessing. It is a place where God's people can meet him.

The church is a place you come to be glad and be blessed. We do not have to go to church to enjoy the Lord. It is always great that we do come to church to uplift someone. You may have a good time in life. If you are saved the best time in your life is coming.

God wants us to overlook what our brother and sister have done to us. We need to get our soul right. One day the Lord will give me a new body. Death is part of life, you were born to die. This is not our home.

We're just passing through. In this world our honor is what judges our life. We can get excited for a ball game and just about anything we like in this world. So why can we not get excited for God. We should know God's house is a place of joy and happiness. When we hear homecoming that should be a time of joy. When the things of this world get me down all I can do is turn to God!

Common Sense

You would think that common sense would let you know that there is a higher power other than yourself. With common sense why do you think people say there is no God. I guess because the devil has blinded their hearts and eyes. If you could say God made a mistake, it was in giving men free will. There are people in this world that just don't believe in God no matter what.

They say you live and die and that's it. There is no God. Only a fool says there is no God. Just think about all the religions in this world. They all try to explain God's work without him. They say death is the end of man. I tell you if you are saved it is only the beginning of the things to come.

If there is not a God where did the stars come from? God is the only one who can put the stars in the sky. He is the only one who can make the sun shine in the day. As smart as man is they still cannot make fruit grow on a tree.

Some say they are not sure if the bible is true. How do you think we can know there is a heaven? We read it in the bible and this word is from God. Heaven goes on forever and ever. We cannot think how big it is. When something is forever that means there is no end. We need to understand God. God's understanding is not our understanding. God's ways are not our ways.

If you are deceived by the devil and his wrong teaching the devil will always have an excuse for you to make it right. He may have you saying, I do not have to go to church. I am already living the good life. There is nothing I need at church. God made Sunday a day of rest. What better way to rest than in the house of God?

The devil's excuses are endless. I am not living good enough for the Lord to save me. Jesus came into this world to die and save the sinner just like you and me. Jesus came into the world for us, but his own received him not. So you use your common sense to follow Jesus and be smart enough to stay out of hell.

Matthew 10:32-33 says "Therefore whoever confess me before men, I will also confess him before my father who is in heaven (33) But whoever denies me before men Him will I also deny before my father who is in heaven. Proverbs 14:12 says "There is a way that seems upright to a man but it's end is the way of death.

Steven W. Edwards

21ST CENTURY

We live in the 21st Century. Many of us can remember when times were different. When we watch the news now there is only bad news. If there was a channel that reported good news no one would watch it. We love to hear bad news. In this country the things being taught about Jesus is in the past. We have turned our backs on God.

We are living in a time were people do not trust each other. Where is the old time love in our heart? On our money it says in God we trust. Do we? What happened to the home of the free, and the home of the brave? This generation is real smart, but we live foolish. We do not serve God. We serve the things around us.

The truth is Jesus still saves souls. If you have not gotten your soul right with him when you die you will go to hell. When Jesus saves your life you are a new creature. Today we have medicine for everything you can think of. This generation is religious, but their hearts are far from God.

A third of the people sitting in church will go to hell. This generation is rich, but unhappy. While we are in this world we should live and enjoy life, but this is a bloody generation. It always for peace but there is no peace. This generation is powerful but it is also weak. We look for hope but our hope is gone. Jesus is our hope he is the only way we should live in this world. In some of our lives Jesus is not there.

Luke 21:26-27 says, "men's hearts fail them from fear and the expectation of those things which are coming on the earth. For the powers of heaven will be shaken. (27) then they will see the Son of Man coming in a cloud with power and great glory. Jeremiah 8:11 says, "for they have healed the hurt of the daughter of my people slightly saying peace! Peace! When there is no peace.

LIVING DAILY

Psalm 61:8 says "So I will sing praise to our name forever, that I may daily perform my vows." When we live daily for God we must get crucified for God daily. The reason Paul was so successful in his walk with God was because he put himself in danger every day. He knew if he did God's work God would take care of him.

The walk with God is daily. Today is the best day of your life. Yesterday is gone, tomorrow is not promised to you. The walk you do each day for God is a praise walk, and a daily walk with God. Just remember what you do today you will have to face it tomorrow.

Cross bearing is a daily decision. Everyone's cross is not the same. Bearing your cross is a sign that you are saved and following the Lord. Pick up your cross and follow me does not mean pick up your problems and follow him. It means do whatever it takes each day to be an example of God's love.

We each have a cross to bear. What is your cross? The cross Jesus is talking about is showing everyone you are a child of God. Ask God daily, "I do not know what is out there Lord, but I want you to go with me." Jesus will never leave you or forsake you. If we leave him he will be right were we left him. In our walk we need to be one mind and one accord in our daily walk. Christians should care for each other. If I cannot lift you up then I am not doing my job. Work now because there will come a time the work you do for Jesus will not matter. When he comes again and gets his children he will take the Holy Spirit with him.

HEART OF STONE

1 Samuel 25:36-39 says, "Now Abigail went to Nabal and he was holding a feast in his house, like the feast of a king. And Nabal's heart was merry within him. For he was very drunk; therefore she told him nothing, little or much, until morning light. (37) So it was in the morning when the wind had gone from Nabal, and his wife had told him these things, that his heart died within him, and he became like stone. (38) Then it happened after about 10 days, that the Lord stuck Nabal, and he died. (39) So when David heard that Nabal was dead, he said Blessed be the Lord who had pleaded the cause of my reproach from the hand of Nabal and has kept his servant from evil. For the Lord has returned the wickedness of Nabal on his own head."

Nabal hardened his own heart then God turned it into stone. Nabal's first sin was being not thankful to

God for what he had done. Do you wonder sometimes why people who are rich or poor just getting by. The bible says God made all our opportunities in our life. He knows who can handle the wealth and who cannot.

The things in our life rich or poor all come from God. Some of us today are just like Nabal unthankful and unholy. These words tell about the ungodly. Many homes are broken up by being selfish. Do not be guilty of saying what is mine. You might own a fine home and it may be all paid for in your name. It's not yours.

You may have a new car or a new pair of shoes but you must remember everything you got belongs to God. Everything you have God can take away in the blink of an eye. The only thing you have in your life is your salvation when you turn your life to God. He said I will be with you even till the end.

You hear people even Christians say look what I got and what I have done. Christians today are too selfish and are evil sinful and ungodly. They are lover of darkness more than light. Just like Nabal we think more of what we eat than about our soul. Just like Nabal ewe live to eat and to drink and be merry. We need to put more on working on the things of God and not so much on the world.

When you die everything you have will go to someone else. Do not miss out on heaven because of your sin and not turning your heart to God because it is never too late until you are dead!

Steven W. Edwards

No Time Zone

God never wants his people to be dumb when it comes to his word the salvation of their life. The promise God has made to his people is when we die and are saved one day we will be in heaven with him. When we die and we are saved one day we will be in heaven.

Once we leave this world their will not be a time zone. This will be a time when men will throw away their watches. God has no time zone. Everyone that is there will know where their mansion is just by asking God. I will have a mind and body like Christ.

When time means nothing God will tell Jesus go get my children, Jesus will give the command for the dead to rise. The lost people will not hear the sound of Jesus saying, "My children come home, and Jesus controls the spiritual air and Holy Spirit.

When I die the Holy Spirit will still be with me in this body. When the command is given even the dead will rise. We come out of the ground when the trumpet sounds. After the word sounds there will still be people left behind. People will still get up and get ready for work. Preachers will get ready to preach. All because they are not saved and did not know Jesus.

Daddy will come from work to no family. The world has never seen anything like this until the rapture comes. All judgement is given to the son. God never made people the same. We will have the body God wants us to have. When we die our body may be in the ground. God will bring the souls with him and then the body and soul will come together. My soul is going to get a new body. Everyone will shout hallelujah glory to the king. The angels will take you to your new mansion.

When you stand before Jesus you will have to give account for the good or bad you have done for is glory. Revelation 5:11 "Then a white robe was given to each of them; and it was said to them that they should rest a little longer until both the number of their fellow servants and their brethren who would be killed as they were was completed.

Revelations 19:6-7 "And I heard as it were a voice of a great multitude as the sound of mighty thundering saying Alleluia! For the Lord God Omnipotent reigns! (7) Let us be glad and rejoice and give him glory for the Marriage of the Lamb has come, and his wife has made herself ready."

Steven W. Edwards

EASED BUT NOT GRIEVED

Amos 6:1-6 "Woe to you who are at ease in Zion, and trust in Mount Samaria, Notable persons in the chief nation, to whom the house of Israel comes. (2) Go over to Calneh and see; and from there go to Hamath the great; then go down to Gath of the Philistines. Are you better than these kingdoms? Is there territory greater than your territory? (3) Woe to you who put far off the day of doom. Who caused the seat of violence to come near.

(4) Who lie on beds of Ivory, stretch out on your couches, Eat lambs from the flock and calves from the midst of the stall; (5) Woe sing idly to the sound of Stringed instruments like David; (6) who drink wine from bowls and anoint yourselves with the best ointments, but are grieved for the affliction of Joseph.

Eased but not grieved this is how most of this

generation are living by a certain tradition but not grieved. We should serve the Lord with gladness and praise who to them that starts a church, but does not make God a part of it. We live in a world that does not like Christians, because we are different because we serve God and not man.

If you walk with God the world will not like you. His word is sharper than a two edge sword, people today have too many gods. They have their money which they put before God. We are no longer known as a Christian nation in the last day. Now everything in this nation we do is okay. We have no more shame in our life.

These days sinners refuse to hear. When Jesus comes back for his children that will not be the end of the world. We should try to be like Jesus, because he never took a short cut. He said what God said. He stood on it. Most preachers today preach what favors man. We could get to church every day if we weren't so lazy.

What happen to the old time music in the church. What is this new music they are playing? We need to get back to the way things were in the old days. Slow down do not do everything so fast. Take time to enjoy what you are doing. If you are saved you should be glad to be called different. When we did our souls will be saved.

Steven W. Edwards

THE TOUCH OF JESUS

Matthew 8:1-4 "When he was come down from the mountain, great multitudes followed him. (2) And, behold, there came a leper and worshipped him, saying, Lord, if thou wilt, thou canst make me clean.(3) And Jesus put forth his hand, and touched him, saying, I will; be thou clean. And immediately his leprosy was cleansed. (4) And Jesus saith unto him, See thou tell no man; but go thy way, shew thyself to the priest, and offer the gift that Moses commanded, for a testimony unto them.

Human beings have five senses for understanding the world around us. The best sense we have is our touch. We touch about a thousand things a day. Jesus has a touch greater than any touch we could ever have. The touch from form the Master is a very special touch. It is a healing touch. One touch from Jesus and the man with leprosy was healed. He had the desire and faith for Jesus to heal him.

Matthew 8:15, " So he touched her hand and the fever left her. and she arose and served them." Jesus touches lives every day. The most important work our Master did was one on one. The bible says God the father is waiting for us to ask him for his touch. Just because we have Jesus in life does not mean we will not have trouble in our life. With just a touch from Jesus a deaf mute will be able to hear.

Mark 7:33 "And he took him aside from the multitude, and put his fingers into his ears, and he spit, and touched his tongue;" Jesus took a lot of bad people in the bible and turned their life to him. He is still doing the same thing today just by his touch,

When Jesus touches you and you get saved you are a new creature, old things become new, we do not do the things we once did. He takes away the disease and he turns darkness into light. Matthew 9:29 "Then he touched their eyes saying according to your faith let it be to you." The same Jesus back then is the same Jesus today. There is no disease or problem that Jesus cannot heal or fix.

WHY I LOVE JESUS

John 21:15-17 "So when they had dined, Jesus saith to Simon Peter, Simon, son of Jonas, lovest thou me more than these? He saith unto him, Yea, Lord; thou knowest that I love thee. He saith unto him, Feed my lambs. (16) He saith to him again the second time, Simon, son of Jonas, lovest thou me? He saith unto him, Yea, Lord; thou knowest that I love thee. He saith unto him, Feed my sheep. (17) He saith unto him the third time, Simon, son of Jonas, lovest thou me? Peter was grieved because he said unto him the third time, Lovest thou me? And he said unto him, Lord, thou knowest all things; thou knowest that I love thee. Jesus saith unto him, Feed my sheep."

I love Jesus for what he has done. He loved me when I was a sinner. I'm glad that I can love him. I'm glad that I can report that God cleaned up my sins. When

Jesus was on the cross he could have called my name. My name was written in the hands of God before I was ever born. He gave me eternal life.

God said before I was born he anointed me to be the son of God. He could have made us like the angels. The angels sit around the throne and praise God. God doesn't send people to hell they send their selves.

I did not put my feet under my daddy's table unless I had at first worked hard every day. On Sunday my mother stopped us from work. In my time there was no money. I remember when I picked cotton for two days and only earned three dollars. When I was 16 or 17 I use to fight other boys for money, and I was good. I would sometimes come home with my eyes shut .My mother would have to feed me.

One day after a fight I went to Amory to a tent revival. The Holy Spirit convicted me of my sins. After that I saw one of the boys I was fighting and told him to come here. He said he didn't want to fight anymore. I didn't want to fight I just wanted to tell someone about what God had done for me. The people that knew me didn't believe me, because my life had been so rough.

When I was 19 I let God have his way in my life. I started preaching, and I went into the army. I preached while I was there too. I have been singing and preaching ever since. God has really been good to me. I just want to thank him. I know no matter what I go through I am not alone. The Holy Spirit is with me. I still get mad and sometimes I make the wrong moves in life. I need God to forgive me daily. I am thankful for him doing that.

He is coming back for me. I will have a new body and a new life. God gives you life, but he also give you death. If you are saved death is a blessing. God is going to change me and make me like him. I will have a body like him and the same power that raised Jesus.

Steven W. Edwards

The hour of Death

We do not like to think about death. I see it a lot but still I never get used to a funeral. Seeing death on the faces of loved ones is hard on my heart. We go to great measure to keep our bodies healthy, be we all have an appointed time to die. Job 14:14 says, " If a man dies shall he live again? All the days of my hard service I will wait till my change comes.

Why do things in life happen the way they do? The secret things in life and in heaven belong to God. God is the giver and taker of life. We cannot do anything about our birth, who our parents are, this is all God's doing. What makes the difference is how we live our life. We are formed from the dust of the earth. When we die the dust is where we will go back.

Why do some people die so young and some live for

over a hundred years? It is because there is no certain time man is promised upon the earth. Life is a mystery. We look at life and we wonder why some children are born with so much difficulties in life. Why aren't all children born healthy?

In the beginning there were no retarded children. The bloodline was almost perfect. God created angels to do his bidding. An Angel can take any form necessary to do the bidding of God. What is death, physical death is the soul separated from the body. Spiritual death is man separated from God.

How much worry does God put on your body after you are dead and gone. When your soul leaves your body. That body will fade away and God will have a new body waiting for you in heaven. There you will live forever.

It is hard for use to imagine forever. No more tears or sorrow or pain. When death comes no one knows the day or the hour. When death comes you will never know so be ready. How many people leave home, kiss their loved one bye going to work, but never make it back. How can I be ready for death by knowing Jesus and the pardoning of your sin. You can face death trusting in God's words. Death to a child of God is a blessing. Some people don't want to die because they love this dirt which we came from. I tell you the body you have now is worth nothing, but the new body you get in heaven will be yours forever! Psalm 74:24. You will guide me with your counsel. And afterward receive me to glory. Psalm 68:28 Your God has commanded your strength Strengthen God What you have done for us. 2 Chronicles 1:9 Now o Lord God, let your promise to David my father be established. For you have made me king over a people like the dust of the earth in multitude.

Steven W. Edwards

ALL I HAVE FOR GOD

Once we were so lost and with no hope. One day we recognized we were nothing and we cried out for help from God. There are times in our life we need to listen to what God is telling us. There are times in our life we feel like giving up and not doing anything. At Christmas do not give a gift to receive a gift. You do it because you love that person. Acts 3:6-7 Then Peter said Silver and gold I do not have, but what I do have I give you: in the name of Jesus Christ of Nazareth rise up and walk. 7- and he took him by the right hand and lifted him up and immediately his feet and ankle bones received strength.

John 18:38 Pilate said to him What is truth? And when he had said this he went out again to the Jews, and said to them, I find no fault in Him at all. Hebrews 11:5 By faith Enoch was taken away so that he did not see death, and was not found. Because God had taken him; for before he was taken he had the testimony that he pleased God.

When you seem to have lost all hope and your health is gone and you have no more money what do you do? First Christians have the truth. The world is a lie. The world does not have anything for you. The world will open up their arms and tell you to look and see what you can get if you just follow the world. Everything in this world has a price. The biggest price is your soul. People today do not want you to hear the truth. Christians have a testimony and it is our sworn duty to be the light in this world. We live in some dark times and bad things are happening to God's people. The best we can do for God we need to do it.

When we stand before God we will have to answer for what we have done and have not done. When you stand before God you will stand by yourself and you will answer about your life and yours only. If you are saved you will not answer for your sins but for your works. How much work do you do for God. It is not how much you do but how much you are willing to do. I take what I have and do what I can to serve God. God will bless the rest to make sure his work gets done That is all God asks of us.

Steven W. Edwards

Christian Talent

Christians have talents and we do not need to hide them. If God gave you a talent he expects you to use it and do not let the devil take your talent. Matthew 25:25-26 And I was afraid and went and hid your talent in the ground. Look there you have what is yours 26- But his lord answered and said to him you wicked and lazy servant. You knew that I reap where I have not sown and gather where I have to scattered seed.

We all today are too lazy to use the talent God has given us. We are afraid of what people might say. It will be worst for you. When God gives you a talent use it! God makes a way out of temptation. If you will just wait. Christians have a talent by paying tithes and offerings. Malachi 3:8 Will a man rob God? Yes you have robed me! But you say in what way have we robbed you? In tithes and offering.

Christians have a trials. When you are going through a trial in life just remember your God owns it all. We have the Lord to fight our battles. Do not be afraid. One day God will give you the victory. When you get the victory do not forget to thank God. Christians have time to give to God. Do not waste it. These times are evil. Children are turning to dope and we have teenage mothers. Homes are being broken. The devil has all kinds of tricks to mess with people head.

Every time the doors to God's house are open you should be flooding in. If the members are not there that place is not a home. 1Peter 4:12-13 12 Beloved, think it not strange concerning the fiery trial which is to try you, as though some strange thing happened unto you: 13 But rejoice, inasmuch as ye are partakers of Christ's sufferings; that, when his glory shall be revealed, ye may be glad also with exceeding joy.

1 Corinthians 10:13 No temptation has overtaken you except what is common to mankind. And God is faithful; he will not let you be tempted beyond what you can bear. But when you are tempted, he will also provide a way out so that you can endure it.

Death Angel

What is evil we call good. We have robbed the poor and we say we won the lottery. We have an abortion and kill our children. We just say my choice. It is my right. Just think about it. If your parents aborted you there would be no you. God gave an angel the power and the tool to be the death angel. That angel got other angels and gave them the same power of death. When will death stop?

One day death will be cast into the lake of fire. Not the angels. What are you going to do when the death angel stands by you. You have to stand before God will you be ready? One day God will tell one of the angels to bring me the lambs of the Book of Life. He will see if your name is in it. When your time is up God will circle your name in the book of life. The death angel will have your location and he will come and get you.

It doesn't matter if you lived a long or short life. When it is time for you to die you will be taken away the same way. Genesis 5:20-24 And all the days of Jared were nine hundred sixty and two years: and he died. 21 And Enoch lived sixty and five years, and begat Methuselah: 22 And Enoch walked with God after he begat Methuselah three hundred years, and begat sons and daughters: 23 And all the days of Enoch were three hundred sixty and five years: 24 And Enoch walked with God: and he was not; for God took him.

Where does your life stand when your time is up? There is a lot of people that play church. There is a difference in going to church and being a part of it. Paul said run the race that is set before you.

2 Kings 2:11 And it came to pass, as they still went on, and talked, that, behold, there appeared a chariot of fire, and horses of fire, and parted them both asunder; and Elijah went up by a whirlwind into heaven.

On Saturday and Sunday there is a lot of people at football games now. Many of them were in church and how many show up at church like they do the games. Are you proud to tell people that you are a Christian. That you love God. Do not be ashamed of God We need to be servants of God. When the death angels comes will you be ready or will you be like the rich man still holding on to the things of this world.

When you are saved you become a member of God's house. What joy will it be when God says Well done.

Steven W. Edwards

It's Time

It's time to let go of your worries. What can cause you to worry at home or at work? Think about it. By worrying it have never made the sick better. There is no medicine for worrying. Nothing is achieved by worrying. It just makes things worst. If you know Jesus as your savior why worry.

I do not know what to do about my bills. Worrying isn't going to pay my bills. It is time to let go of my worrying by prayer. You cannot cross the bridge by yourself. God is with you just pray. Do not worry. You are in the hands of the almighty God.

It is time to let go of your old wounds, anger, and sin. This is hard to do sometimes. We could be wounded by family and friends. God can forgive you first. You must forgive those who wronged you. God said bind up the wounds and give it all to him. I have been hurt. I just think about what Jesus had to go through. He did nothing, but he hurt for our sins.

What about his father he had to turn his back on his son because of the sins he place on Jesus's back. By confession to God he will take all of your sins away. The devil picks sin out. That is how he gets you to sin.

Hebrew 12:1-2 Wherefore seeing we also are compassed about with so great a cloud of witnesses, let us lay aside every weight, and the sin which doth so easily beset us, and let us run with patience the race that is set before us, 2 Looking unto Jesus the author and finisher of our faith; who for the joy that was set before him endured the cross, despising the shame, and is set down at the right hand of the throne of God.

Proverbs 12:25 Heaviness in the heart of man maketh it stoop: but a good word maketh it glad. Psalm 55:22 Cast thy burden upon the Lord, and he shall sustain thee: he shall never suffer the righteous to be moved.

Psalm 104:13-14 He watereth the hills from his chambers: the earth is satisfied with the fruit of thy works. 14 He causeth the grass to grow for the cattle, and herb for the service of man: that he may bring forth food out of the earth;

OUR MIND

What is on your mind? We look at what we got in the bank. Our Credit cards to see how much we can give. At Christmas we give gifts because the wise men gave gifts to Jesus but do not go into debt trying to buy things you cannot afford. So many people will not be able to gets gifts for people they love, because they have no money.

What we have is because God give it to you. Whatever you give you cannot out give God. Every need we have God will meet. We need to do more for God this year. Life is not built on a dollar bill. We try to have everything like other people we see. We do not know how much debt these people are in. What are you going to do with the rest of your time this year?

How much time do you waste watching tv? How is your faith this year? Are you faithful in your service to

God? God's people need to be busy for God. In whatever way he wants us to be. Are you going to keep going the way you have this year or are you ready for a change?

Genesis 31:15-16 Are we not counted of him strangers? for he hath sold us, and hath quite devoured also our money. 16 For all the riches which God hath taken from our father, that is ours, and our children's: now then, whatsoever God hath said unto thee, do.

Psalm 15:5 He that putteth not out his money to usury, nor taketh reward against the innocent. He that doeth these things shall never be moved.

Alleluia

When someone says Alleluia what does it mean? It means praise ye the Lord, in God's word it has Alleluia 24 times. Revelation 19:1-8 And after these things I heard a great voice of much people in heaven, saying, Alleluia; Salvation, and glory, and honour, and power, unto the Lord our God: 2 For true and righteous are his judgments: for he hath judged the great whore, which did corrupt the earth with her fornication, and hath avenged the blood of his servants at her hand.

3 And again they said, Alleluia And her smoke rose up for ever and ever.

4 And the four and twenty elders and the four beasts fell down and worshipped God that sat on the throne, saying, Amen; Alleluia.

5 And a voice came out of the throne, saying, Praise our

God, all ye his servants, and ye that fear him, both small and great.

6 And I heard as it were the voice of a great multitude, and as the voice of many waters, and as the voice of mighty thunderings, saying, Alleluia: for the Lord God omnipotent reigneth.

7 Let us be glad and rejoice, and give honour to him: for the marriage of the Lamb is come, and his wife hath made herself ready.

8 And to her was granted that she should be arrayed in fine linen, clean and white: for the fine linen is the righteousness of saints

We are going to look at 6 Alleluia found in the bible the first on is the Alleluia of Creation and providence. It tells more about it in Psalm 104. God has made all things both heaven and earth. God has placed everything in life which we see or eat. God said it was good. Just think what life would be like without the trees. All the things we use but never think about all God made he made for our enjoyment.

The second Alleluia is the Alleluia of life. The Jews began with Abraham. God has provided and watched over the few until they became many. When Jesus comes back there will not be any more Holy Spirit in the world. Those who are left behind will beg and most will accept the mark of the beast.

The third alleluia will be the alleluia of Grace. By grace are you saved. You cannot get grace at a store. You cannot sell it to get something else. You only get grace by God. God is loving and merciful. The fourth Alleluia is of eternity because one day when we die we will be in eternity with God. No more getting sick and no more dying.

The fifth alleluia of praise will be able to sing and praise and praise God for the rest of our life which will be forever. The sixth Alleluia is the Alleluia of Judgement. One day we will stand before God and will be judged. If we did God's work like we was told to do we will say Alleluia and we will give thanks to the Almighty God.

WHY WAS JESUS BORN

Jesus was born in Bethlehem to fulfill prophesy. Michah 5:2 but you Bethelehem Ephrathah though you are little among thousands, of Judah yet out of you shall come forth to me the one to be ruler in Israel Whose going forth are from of old from everlasting.

Luke2:10-11 And the angel said unto them, Fear not: for, behold, I bring you good tidings of great joy, which shall be to all people. 11 For unto you is born this day in the city of David a Saviour, which is Christ the Lord.

Before God ever created the earth he always knew his son would be a ransom for the world and their sins. Why was Jesus born in such a small town and not some bigger place? This is where God wanted it to happen to fulfill the prophesy. Jesus was born so we might see God through his Son. Anyone who has seen Jesus has seen

God. When Jesus comes into our life we look different. We will act different so let your light shine. Jesus was born to defeat the devil who has power over death. One day death and hell will be cast into the lake of fire. God made Luther the death angel because of the people's sins. In heaven there will be no blind or any sick people. Mark 3:27 No one can enter into the strong man's house and plunder his goods unless he first binds the strong man. Then he will plunder his house.

1 Peter 2:24 Who himself bore our sins in his own body on the tree that we having died to sins might live for righteousness by whose stripes you are healed. Jesus was born and died for our sins. It was all in God's plans. God love and the need of love is the kind of love we should have for one another. Remember Jesus is the reason for the seadon.

WAYS TO MISS HEAVEN

These are the things that keep a person form being born again. Proverbs 14:12 There is a way that seems right to a man, but it ends is the way of death." Many people will say I'm a church member and have been one for a long time so I'm fine. These things will keep us from going to heaven. It does not matter how long you are going to church. Are you saved? Going to church will help you grow. This is a spiritual growth so you can be more like Christ. Your light can get bigger and bigger so everyone can see. The next thing that can keep you from getting saved is when we say we are doing the best we can. You cannot be good enough to go to heaven. The next thing is trusting in others. Being in a certain club or going to a certain church will not get you to heaven.

You cannot mix righteousness and unrighteousness

together. The two do not have any business together. No matter how good it sounds. The next thing you do is putting your trust in riches. It does not matter how much money you have or how much you give to the church or to other people. That will not get you to heaven. No matter how much you give you cannot out give God. If God's people will give God what belongs to him there is no telling how much God would bless them.

The next thing you do is trusting in good works. You cannot do enough good works to get to heaven. Before I was born God know my name and knew what day I would give my life to him. Only the saved and redeemed will be in the Lambs book of life. Jesus took the book out of the fathers hands. He died for it. Every time you pray or every time you tell someone about Jesus it's in the book. The next thing we do is trusting that we will have the next day or the next hour to turn our life to God. I will give my life to God but not today. Do it today because there might not be tomorrow for you. If we believe in Christ and confess in our heart we will be saved. Mark 1:4-5 John did baptize in the wilderness, and preach the baptism of repentance for the remission of sins. 5 And there went out unto him all the land of

Judaea, and they of Jerusalem, and were all baptized of him in the river of Jordan, confessing their sins.

John 1:11-13 He came to his own and his own did not receive him. But as many as received him to them he gave the right to become children of God. Who are born not of blood nor of the will of the flesh nor of the will of man but of God.

Steven W. Edwards

New Year's Vow

The clock is ticking the new year will be here soon. What is a vow? It is a solemn pledge or promise especially to God for the desire to do better. As we go in this new year what vow will you give to God. God does not want you to make foolish vows you cannot keep. What we need to vow is to stay separate form sin. No Christian can live in sin and for God at the same.

Psalm 76:11 Vow, and pay unto the Lord your God: let all that be round about him bring presents unto him that ought to be feared. Daniel 1:8 But Daniel purposed in his heart that he would not defile himself with the portion of the king's meat, nor with the wine which he drank: therefore he requested of the prince of the eunuchs that he might not defile himself.

Sometimes in life we must give up some things we like so we can keep our vows to God. Only God knows what the new year will hold. This year you may have had a lot of bad times and it was a struggle to live. There was a struggle in the church and even more of a struggle at home. Maybe next year we will turn around in America. Maybe the job market will pick up and maybe they will get rid of same sex marriage.

God's people should say enough is enough of all the sin and wicked ways of this year. The next thing we need to do is vow to serve God when he needs you to. In our everyday life if we would only chose the way of God and everything else will come to you.

Most people will get upset if their favorite team loses or for some reason they cannot play their game. Why don't we get upset about people not going to church or why people do not serve God. The next vow is the vow of stewardship no person is a good Christian unless you have a stewardship to God.

1 Corinthians 9:17-18 For if I do this thing willingly, I have a reward: but if against my will, a dispensation of the gospel is committed unto me. 18 What is my reward then? Verily that, when I preach the gospel, I may make the gospel of Christ without charge, that I abuse not my power in the gospel.

Tithing is between that person and God if you vow your vow on tithing and you give like you are supposed to God will multiply what you give. Next year remember God is the Master of it all. God has been good to us. When you vow a vow go God you need to keep it. You do not have to tell anyone just tell God what you are going to do. Do it, but do not make a vow to God if you do not plan to do it.

Steven W. Edwards

Three Precious Jewels

Isaiah 43:1 but now thus says the Lord who created you O Jacob, and he who formed you O Israel fear not for I have redeemed you. I have called you by your name; you are mine." The first precious jewel is that God has redeemed the lost of their sin, and has the power to forgive sin. When we came from our mother a sinner and then one day the Holy Spirit told us there was a way out. He forgave us of sin and I thank God that the price has been paid for our sin. After you turn your life to God you will never be a slave of the devil again. We will be a new creature in Christ.

The next precious jewel is God knows who I am. John 10:27 "My sheep hear my voice and I know them and they follow me." One day when I die God will say well done my faithful servant. I put you over small things on earth and now I will put you over many things.

He knows who I am and where I am. When he needs me he will call me by name. God might need you to tell someone about him or maybe he wants you to show Christ to someone. The next precious jewel that God gives is that you belong to God. He loved the church so much that he gave his life for it. One day he will come again and take us out of this sinful and painful world and take us to heaven. When we get to heaven the gates of heaven will never close and we will never know sin anymore.

One day is coming I can shut my eyes in perfect peace, because he knows me and has saved me. My mind cannot think how God thinks because God is all knowing. My heart cannot feel and my eyes cannot see the things God has for us. I know thy are mine and I have called thee. We are one in the Lord. We are brothers and sisters in Christ.

My treasure is laid up there somewhere beyond the blue sky. I got a book filled with my name in it and all I have done. We have did some dumb things in our life, but the smartest thing you did was let Christ in your life the greatest treasure you could ever have.

WHEN THE SHADOWS GATHERS

Life is filled with unexpected trials and problems which sometimes get the best of us. Life is a vapor that appears for a time and then fades away. Life is what you make out of it. There are many in this world like dogs. When they throw up they go back and eat what is left behind. What I mean is once they get rid of all the bad in their life they go right back and pick it up.

Everyone has a destiny we all must follow. Your days are numbered so do not waste time not following God or always going the wrong way. Sometimes the wrong things in life seem so right at the time. After you see it is wrong you wonder why you did that in the first place.

Sometimes life can seem to be joyous and then comes a bad shadow and takes all your joy away. Many of times the shadow that comes to us is our own fault.

The path you choose will determine the outcome of your journey. The people in our life that want us to look bad no matter if you are doing good or not. They mean you no good. They do not know the power of God. You keep praying that God will open their eyes. What death seems to be the shadow of death is darkness. In the shadow there is calmness and cool the sheep enjoy the shadow, in the shadow they have no fear will come to us.

If we know Jesus we should have no worries because we will have a new home and a new body. If you do not know Jesus then that shadow is a big problem. The bible said there will be souls crying out from under the altar. When we lay down our earthly vessel and we are saved we will be with Jesus. When Jesus was dead he went to hell and preached to the lost.

You today have a living soul and it is a breathe form god. Your soul is no different from my soul. God loves all souls. The soul does not control the body. The soul does not sin. The things I should not do I do, and what I should do I fine hard to do. What death seems to be it seem to be just ashes to ashes and dust to dust, but that is only what happens to the body not the soul.

We all travel different paths in life, but the end we all have one choice that is the same to believe in Jesus. The soul that is not saved it will go to hell. Wait until the day of judgement. When the soul gets to heaven they will see it all and hear it all. Body and soul will be united. I will have a new body and a new life. Paul said the angels in heaven sit around and cheer for the people that are still fighting the good fight for God. God will be God and able to do what he wants to do. When I'm down he can pick me up. When I need a friend he will be that friend.

With all your enemies around you God will make sure not one hair on your head is touched. What can we be. We can be the best shadow over this bad land the world has ever seen when the world is too much there is a God waiting to help.

Steven W. Edwards

Encouragement

We need encouragement and how we get it is through the house of God. We come to the house of God for a blessing. We need to thank Jesus everyday not just on Sunday Deuteronomy 28:6 Blessed shalt thou be when thou comest in, and blessed shalt thou be when thou goest out.

We need to thank God we are born again and washed in the blood of the lamb. We have God's unfailing love. God loves us and will always love us. We find love in this world is something we cannot always count on . God's love and grace we can always count on. 2 Corinthians 12:7-10 And lest I should be exalted above measure through the abundance of the revelations, there was given to me a thorn in the flesh, the messenger of Satan to buffet me, lest I should be exalted above measure. 8 For this thing I besought the

Lord thrice, that it might depart from me. 9 And he said unto me, My grace is sufficient for thee: for my strength is made perfect in weakness. Most gladly therefore will I rather glory in my infirmities, that the power of Christ may rest upon me. 10 Therefore I take pleasure in infirmities, in reproaches, in necessities, in persecutions, in distresses for Christ's sake: for when I am weak, then am I strong.

Jeremiah 23:2-3 2 Therefore thus saith the Lord God of Israel against the pastors that feed my people; Ye have scattered my flock, and driven them away, and have not visited them: behold, I will visit upon you the evil of your doings, saith the Lord. 3 And I will gather the remnant of my flock out of all countries whither I have driven them, and will bring them again to their folds; and they shall be fruitful and increase.

There are times we find ourselves running someone down. We as Christians need to try to pick up people when they get down give them a good word of encouragement. That good word may lead them to Jesus, but bad words may lead them far away. Just remember your strength comes from the Lord. No matter what we go through God is with us. He is our shepherd and we are his sheep. He will provide everything in this life and the life to come.

God speaks to us when we need it. Jesus said I'm with you always even till death. When Jesus comes you need to have your soul ready. These bad days will come before Jesus. One day he will take us from this world. The joy of Heaven we have. I tell you today there is no way to heaven but by the blood of Jesus. Death to Christians mean that the devil has already been overcome. The same power that raised Jesus will raise you because the power and grace of God. Sometimes in your life we have let downs and disappointments, but do not let that get you down. You have Jesus

Steven W. Edwards

THE ABC'S OF JESUS

We will be looking at the letters A, B, C, of Jesus. Today we are just going to use the letter B. Jesus is all and all. We should know him and enjoy him. We should enjoying telling other about him. Revelation 22:13-14 13 I am Alpha and Omega, the beginning and the end, the first and the last. 14 Blessed are they that do his commandments, that they may have right to the tree of life, and may enter in through the gates into the city.

The first B we will look at is balm. A balm is a fragrant ointment that soothes, comforts, and heals. Jeremiah 8:22 Is there no balm in Gilead; is there no physician there? why then is not the health of the daughter of my people recovered?" Jesus is the balm. We see all these murders and sin practiced right in our streets and in our homes every day without any care at all and we see these things and we ask is there healing for a child of God?

I say there is healing. His name is Jesus. He is there every time something is going on. He is the only physician there I no other doctor better than Jesus. The next B is the bright and morning star. When the shepherd saw the star they rejoiced. There is no start in heaven brighter than Jesus. I always know he is there.

The next B is the builder of the church on all the other ground I stand is sinking. One day we will be called up to heaven to meet Jesus. You have never had a greater meal till you eat off of Jesus table. He is the bread which came down from heaven. Jesus is the bread of life. If we have this bread we do not want in this world.

The word of God has a great taste. When we get a new body God will take care of it. Our new body will not get dirty or turn to dust. I will have a perfect body. The time is coming when I will look good all the time. Mathew 2:10 When they saw the star, they rejoiced with exceeding great joy." John 6:32-33 Then Jesus said unto them, Verily, verily, I say unto you, Moses gave you not that bread from heaven; but my Father giveth you the true bread from heaven. 33 For the bread of

God is he which cometh down from heaven, and giveth life unto the world.

Hebrew 1:3-4 Who being the brightness of his glory, and the express image of his person, and upholding all things by the word of his power, when he had by himself purged our sins, sat down on the right hand of the Majesty on high: 4 Being made so much better than the angels, as he hath by inheritance obtained a more excellent name than they." Revelation 19:7 Let us be glad and rejoice, and give honour to him: for the marriage of the Lamb is come, and his wife hath made herself ready.

Steven W. Edwards

Last Judgement

The last trial on the earth is coming. Time on earth will have ended. The thousand year millennium time period will be over. The New Jerusalem that John saw coming out of heaven has already been set on the new earth. The resurrection of the church and the resurrection of man is about one thousand and seven years.

We have already enjoyed the new Jerusalem. We have already enjoyed the thousand year millennium period. We have enjoyed the things God has given us to do. Then comes the last trial. The new body we have in this New Jerusalem that sets on this new earth surrounded by this new heaven is a timeless thing.

One day one eternal day while we have enjoyed the blessing of God and time has rolled on that thousand years those who are in hell have suffered so bad. Words cannot tell you about how much they suffered and they have suffered day by day and hour by hour, and week by week, month by month. When all of this is over with and the white throne judgement is over,

Everyone that is cast in the lake of fire will be weeping and gnashing of teeth. There will be no weeping and gnashing of teeth. They will not have the peace of everlasting peace. The man that was tormented by the flames will get a chance to stand before the white throne of Judgement. They will stand before the almighty God and give account of everything he has ever done. He did not turn his life to Jesus. He treated people bad who tried to tell him about Jesus. He was lost and set to hell and is doomed forever and ever. He will not be by himself.

Revelation 20:11 And I saw a great white throne, and him that sat on it, from whose face the earth and the heaven fled away; and there was found no place for them." Jesus is the judge and he is sitting on the white throne. Everybody in hell is being brought up to stand before the King of Kings. He will send them into everlasting darkness.

God did not prepare hell for you and me or any person he made. God made hell for the devil and his angels. After man sinned and came short of the glory of God and death passed upon all men. Men would not honor Jesus his son as a personal savior. God said reach this is such a permanent place for those who refuse to refuse my son. We look to him for salvation. Those who will not put their sins under his blood.

Those who will not seek the face of Jesus will find themselves in hell. Jesus is sitting on the throne and power and the right to judge has been given him by the father. Now all those who spit in his face and mocked him and beat him will stand before Jesus and get judged.

We need to think about the lost people that do not know Jesus. Hell is a breathe away. We got people in this world that are lost and going to hell. We are not doing anything about it. One day they will stand before Jesus. They will be cast into the lake of fire and you did or said nothing to help them. Jesus is just one prayer away. Will you let Jesus into your life today.

Steven W. Edwards

Ask Yourself

What would you think Jesus would think. He would always think positive. Are you positive or negative thinking? Jesus thought positive in everything he did or said. Philippians 4:8-9 Finally, brethren, whatsoever things are true, whatsoever things are honest, whatsoever things are just, whatsoever things are pure, whatsoever things are lovely, whatsoever things are of good report; if there be any virtue, and if there be any praise, think on these things. 9 Those things, which ye have both learned, and received, and heard, and seen in me, do: and the God of peace shall be with you.

Do you think positive about the church or do you always focus on the negative side of the church. A Christian should always think positive. Jesus is on our side. Jesus wants our best faith because faith brings victory. 1 John 5:4 For whatsoever is born of God overcometh the world: and this is the victory that overcometh the world, even our faith."

Paul was the positive thinking person outside of Jesus. Paul was in prison and was still praising God. While he was in prison he wrote a lot of the books of the bible. Paul knew no matter what Jesus was going to take care of him. A positive thinking person is happier than a negative thinking person. A negative thinking person cannot be happy. They are always thinking about the bad that is going to come.

A positive thinking person knows that even when they have fallen as low as they can go Jesus will pick them up. Hear the Holy Spirit in your life. Isaiah 55:3 Incline your ear, and come unto me: hear, and your soul shall live; and I will make an everlasting covenant with you, even the sure mercies of David."

When the world turns their backs on me and you God is always there. The things Jesus listen to will lift up heaven. Our eyes are the window to our soul. Our eyes display how we are to the world. What do you let your eye hear. Many people try to live in the middle of the fence. I say get on one side or the other. Serve God or serve the devil. You cannot serve both at the same time.

Praise and cursing do no come from the same mouth. Do not listen to people saying bad words out of their mouths.

Sometimes things around you are not always great. Just remember Jesus is with you always. There is no problem too big for Jesus. Jesus looks for the good of others. Jesus never looked at someone's faults. He always looked at the good. Do you look for the good in people?

What would Jesus say? Matthew 12:34-35 O generation of vipers, how can ye, being evil, speak good things? for out of the abundance of the heart the mouth speaketh. 35 A good man out of the good treasure of the heart bringeth forth good things: and an evil man out of the evil treasure bringeth forth evil things."

Some people speak hard and unkind words to others. Jesus spoke forgiveness of sins! Why is it that most people like to hear bad things instead of good. What would Jesus do? Hebrews 13:21 Make you perfect in every good work to do his will, working in you that which is wellpleasing in his sight, through Jesus Christ; to whom be glory for ever and ever. Amen."

Steven W. Edwards

TRUMAN L. CARTER II

Truman, died too young, but it was God's will. It was God's will to call him home, but while he was here he touched so many lives. He did it in so many ways. My son When he found about he had pancreatic cancer, about three years ago he approached it with a positive attitude. He once stated, "Whether I go, or whether I stay I'm a winner either way." He won the victory at 9:37am, Thursday October 26, 2014. He was being treated at The Cancer Centers of America Southeast Hospital in Newnan Georgia.

Truman was born in Amory Mississippi on May 4, 1963 to Truman L. Carter and Josephine Herndon Carter Howard. He grew up there in Amory, Mississippi and in Hamilton , Alabama. He graduated from Hatley High School in 1982. While attending Hatley High we has named Mr. Hatley and elected class president. He was the man with the plan to make school cool.

He was member of Carnation Baptist Church in Okolona Mississippi. He always wanted to be in Law enforcement. was Deputy Sheriff in Tupelo Mississippi. He was a longtime beloved Lee County Deputy Sheriff, and an all-around good man. At the time of his death he had served 19 years in law enforcement. He won numerous citation awards. He was tough, but compassionate and drew high marks for his service to his fellowman.

Truman was a born musician, songwriter, and performer. He enjoyed fishing loved the local fish eateries. He was a great southern storyteller and avid conversationalist. He has been sorely missed by all.

RICHARD H. CARTER

Richard H. Carter was always sick growing up, but he still had a good life. He found the Lord at an early age. Just like his brother he loved the Lord and loved playing music for him and making people happy.

I know that both of them are in Heaven right now playing music for God. There is no more pain or sorrow for him, no worries about tomorrow because there is no time in Heaven. I can hear him saying,

I went home, yes I miss my family down there. I miss the love we had, but I'm with God now so don't be sad. My God Dad if you could just see the sights. If you could see how my life has changed, it's just how we talked about and a whole lot more. We will be together again. Don't cry, I'm with Jesus. So I'm just fine. Goodbye for now, but not for long.

Steven W. Edwards

www.ingramcontent.com/pod-product-compliance
Lightning Source LLC
Chambersburg PA
CBHW030328080526
44584CB00012B/755